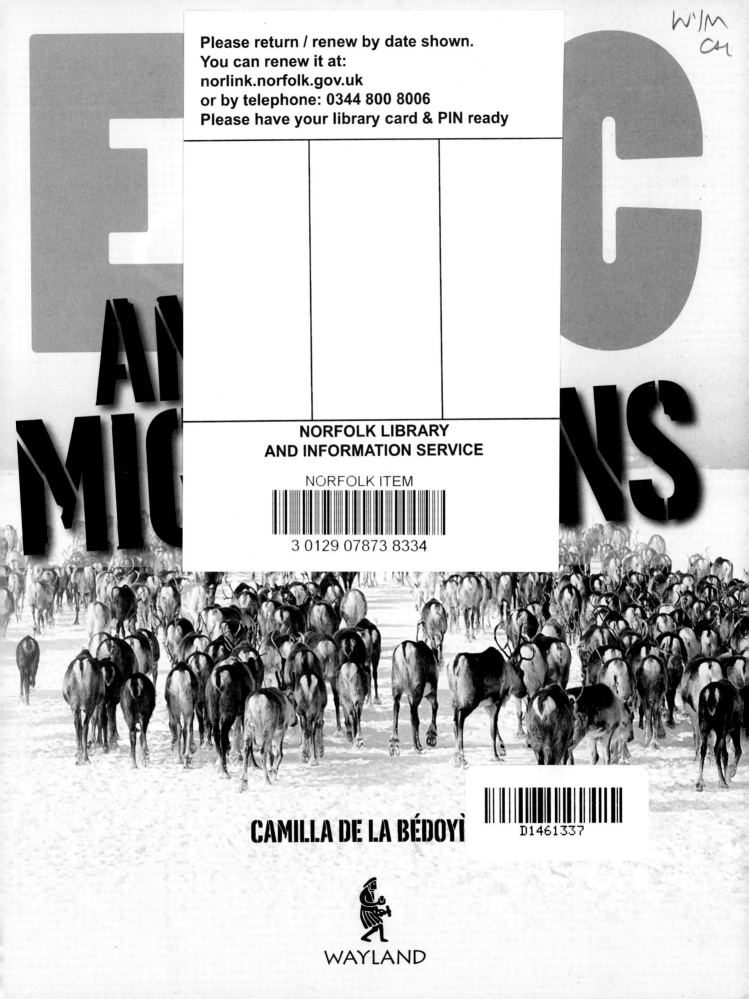

CAMILLA DE LA BÉDOYÈ

WAYLAND

CONTENTS

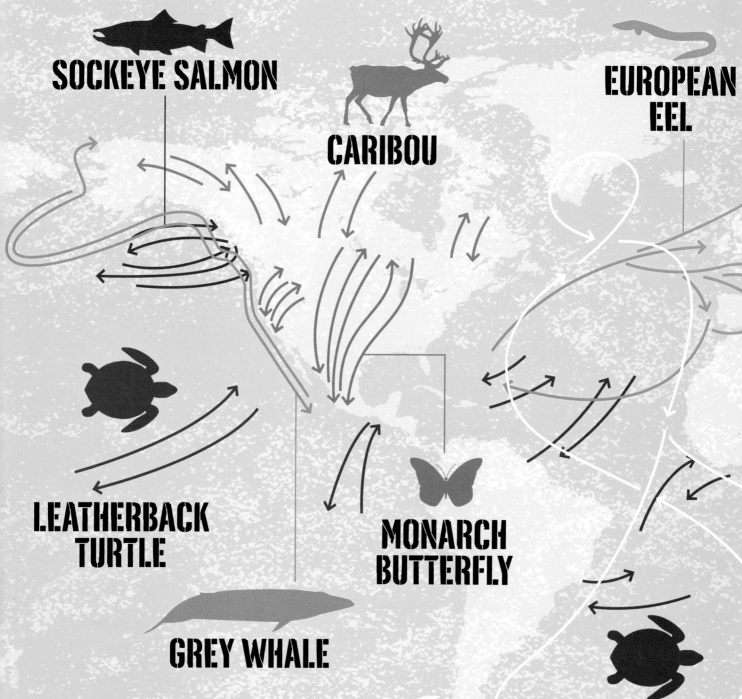

SOCKEYE SALMON

CARIBOU

EUROPEAN EEL

LEATHERBACK TURTLE

MONARCH BUTTERFLY

GREY WHALE

LEATHERBACK TURTLE

ZOOPLANKTON

ARCTIC TERN

CARIBOU

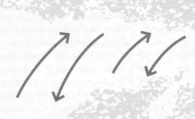

WILDEBEEST

DRAGONFLY

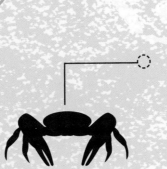

CHRISTMAS ISLAND RED CRAB

STRAW-COLOURED FRUIT BAT

LEATHERBACK TURTLE

INTRODUCTION

Massive animal migrations are some of nature's most inspiring events. Animals of all shapes and sizes undertake incredible journeys to avoid harsh winters or in search of breeding grounds and feeding areas.

Migrations play a vital role in the ecosystem, connecting very varied habitats. Some animals find their way across treacherous terrain or swim or fly thousands of kilometres with amazing accuracy, returning to exactly the same spot year after year. Others undertake incredible journeys only once, for example sockeye salmon return to their birthplace after a lifetime at sea.

In many instances, scientists still do not know exactly how animals migrate. Some animals may be able to detect Earth's magnetic field and use it as a compass. Others may use the sun to find their way, while others are taught the route by parents and other members of their group.

Many species have followed the same migration routes in huge herds for thousands of years. Some animals, such as sharks, make the same journey several times a year, often travelling alone.

Every year, millions of sockeye salmon travel inland on an ambitious migration, which can involve swimming up to 1,600 km (1,000 miles) from the Pacific Ocean back to the freshwater lake where they were born, only to breed and die. In doing so, they must navigate rapids and waterfalls, climbing to lakes that can be 1,950 m (6,400 ft) above sea level.

SOME ANIMALS MIGRATE THOUSANDS OF KILOMETRES, WHILE OTHERS TRAVEL A FEW METRES.

MONARCH BUTTERFLY

EPIC INSECT JOURNEY

Where	Between Canada and Mexico
When	Autumn and spring
Why	In search of a mild winter
How	Flying and gliding

A monarch butterfly weighs no more than a pea, but each year it makes a staggering journey across the whole continent of North America.

In September, millions of monarch butterflies start an incredible migration. They descend on the pine trees of a Mexican forest, and hibernate there over the winter. When spring arrives, they wake and head north to their feeding grounds, where they mate and lay their eggs.

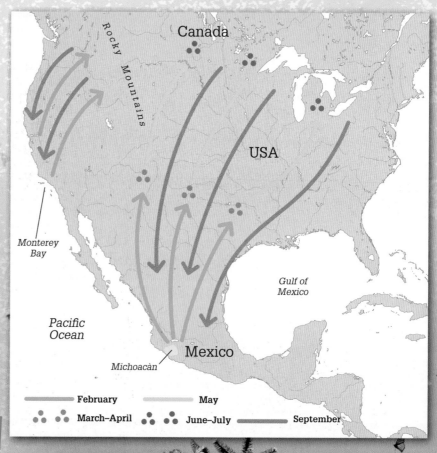

Rocky Mountains

Canada

USA

Monterey Bay

Pacific Ocean

Michoacàn

Mexico

Gulf of Mexico

▬▬ February	▬▬ May	
•• March–April	•• June–July	▬▬ September

Monarch caterpillars feed on toxic milkweed plants and become poisonous too. The poison stays in their bodies, protecting them from predators.

TIMELINE

FEBRUARY

Monarchs come out of hibernation in Mexico and head north to mate.

MARCH–APRIL

Eggs are laid on milkweed plants in the USA, and these hatch into caterpillars.

A MONARCH CAN TRAVEL ABOUT 45 KM (28 MILES) A DAY.

There are two populations of migrating monarchs in North America. One population lives west of the Rocky Mountains and spends the winter in California's Monterey Bay. The other, larger population lives on the American plains east of the Rocky Mountains, and spends the winter in a small area of pine forests in Michoacàn, Mexico.

The winter home of monarchs was a mystery until the 1970s, when scientists tagged individual butterflies and volunteers helped to track their route **to forests in Mexico.**

UP TO 350 MILLION MONARCHS REACH THEIR WINTER HOMES IN MEXICO AND CALIFORNIA.

MIGRATION MYSTERY

How do fragile insects find their way from the USA and Canada to a small area of Mexican forest? Scientists think they use a range of clues, such as the sun, magnetic fields and smell. They also seem to use landmarks, such as the Rocky Mountains, to guide them.

MAY

The caterpillars pupate and emerge as adults ready to fly north and lay more eggs.

JUNE – JULY

The butterflies arrive in their summer home and lay two more generations of eggs.

SEPTEMBER

The fourth generation of butterflies emerge from pupae but do not die. They migrate south and hibernate over the winter.

WILDEBEEST

TREK AROUND AFRICA

Where	East African grasslands
When	All year
Why	For better grazing grounds
How	Walking, running, swimming

The wildebeest migration has occurred for more than a million years and is an amazing sight on the African plains.

The mass movement of wildebeest, a type of antelope, attracts tourists – and predators – throughout the year. These animals are always on the go, as they follow the rains and move from one grazing area to another. The migrating herds nibble at fresh shoots of grass. In doing so, they help to maintain a vast African landscape that supports many other animals.

HERDS TRAVEL THROUGH THE YEAR, IN A SLOW CLOCKWISE CIRCLE, FOR MORE THAN 2,900 KM (1,800 MILES).

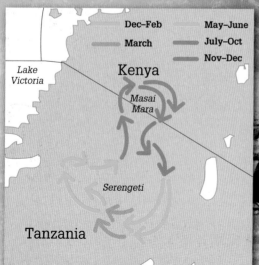

Dec–Feb	May–June
March	July–Oct
	Nov–Dec

Lake Victoria

Kenya

Masai Mara

Serengeti

Tanzania

TIMELINE

DEC–FEB

Females give birth on the south-eastern plains of the Serengeti during the wet season.

MARCH

The herds begin their migration, heading north-west towards Lake Victoria.

A WILDEBEEST RUNS AT 80 KM/H (50 MPH).

The wildebeest are not alone when they migrate. A number of other grazing animals – including zebras, Thomson's gazelles and elands – also enjoy safety in numbers and travel with them. The herds visit grazing areas that are rich in phosphorous, a mineral that is essential for their health.

MIGRATION MYSTERY

The herds do not follow an identical route every year, and scientists are not sure how they choose which route to follow. It seems that the animals may learn routes from year to year, and they also head in the direction of thunderstorms and rainfall, which they see on the horizon.

Wildebeest stay in huge herds because it is a safer way to migrate. Predators, such as cheetahs, find it harder to attack a large, confusing group of animals than a lone traveller.

1.3 MILLION BLUE WILDEBEEST UNDERTAKE THE WORLD'S LARGEST LAND MIGRATION.

Up to half a million calves are born in just two weeks. Only one in every six calves survives its first year. Migrating wildebeest share their habitat with many predators, including **lions and spotted hyenas.**

MAY–JUNE
They arrive at their grazing grounds and mate.

JULY–OCT
The herds travel north to the Masai Mara in the dry season.

NOV–DEC
The herds trek southwards back towards the Serengeti to complete the circuit.

ARCTIC TERN

RECORD-BREAKING FLIER

Where	**Between the Arctic and Antarctic**
When	**July to November, April to June**
Why	**For food**
How	**Flying**

For migrating animals, the shortest distance between two points is not always a straight line.

Arctic terns regularly migrate between the Arctic, near the North Pole, and Antarctica, near the South Pole. If they travelled in a straight line the route would be 15,000 km (9,000 miles). However, these globe-trotters fly in a figure-of-eight to make the most of prevailing winds and save energy. Each bird's round trip actually covers an incredible 70,000 km (43,000 miles).

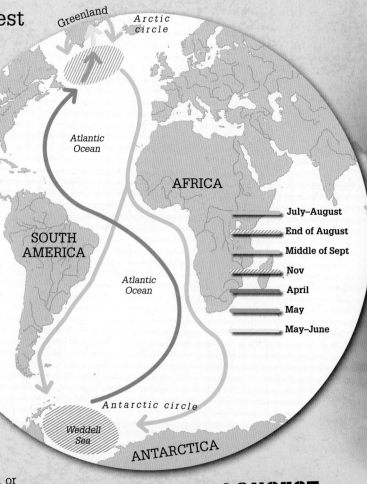

Greenland
Arctic circle
Atlantic Ocean
AFRICA
SOUTH AMERICA
Atlantic Ocean

	July–August
	End of August
	Middle of Sept
	Nov
	April
	May
	May–June

Antarctic circle
Weddell Sea
ANTARCTICA

Arctic terns feed at sea by skimming fish from near the water's surface, or plunging head-first into the water to grab crustaceans in their beaks.

THIS IS THE LONGEST REGULAR MIGRATION OF ANY BIRD.

JULY–AUGUST
The birds leave their breeding sites in Greenland, near the North Pole.

END OF AUGUST
They spend a month at a stop-over point in the middle of the North Atlantic to feed.

MIDDLE OF SEPTEMBER
The birds head south. Some fly down the north-west coast of Africa, some head across the Atlantic and down the coast of South America.

ARCTIC TERNS SPEND MORE HOURS IN THE SUNLIGHT THAN ANY OTHER BIRD.

Arctic terns are almost unique among animals because they experience both the Arctic summer and the Antarctic summer. Chicks hatch in the Arctic breeding grounds and grow fast so that they are ready to begin the long flight to the Antarctic. When the terns head south they cover about 330 km (205 miles) a day, but they can travel up to 670 km (416 miles) every day on the return flight!

MIGRATION MYSTERY

How do migrating birds find their way, often across continents or, in the case of the Arctic tern, across the planet? Scientists have been trying to solve this mystery for decades. One theory is that birds can detect the magnetic field produced by Earth, and use it as a compass to find north. They probably also use other clues, such as the position of the sun and landmarks, as well as learning routes from older birds.

When they reach the Antarctic, the terns feast on vast amounts of food. There are huge swarms of Antarctic krill (small, shrimp-like crustaceans) in the Weddell Sea in the southern summer, **which draw many animals to the region.**

IN ITS LIFETIME, EACH BIRD TRAVELS THE EQUIVALENT OF FLYING THREE TIMES TO THE MOON.

NOV
They reach the Weddell Sea, in the Antarctic.

APRIL
They leave the Antarctic and head back to the Arctic, flying in a massive 'S' shape to follow the winds.

MAY
Some birds take a break at the stop-over point in the North Atlantic.

MAY–JUNE
The birds reach Greenland to rest and breed.

CARIBOU

ACROSS THE FROZEN NORTH

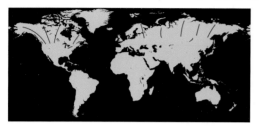

Where	Between tundra and forests
When	Spring and autumn
Why	For grazing and breeding
How	Walking, running, swimming

Caribou face driving snow and wolves as they battle through harsh northern landscapes.

Life in the cold north is hard, and food is not always easy to find. It is hunger – and the need to find good, nutritious food – that urges some caribou to go on an annual migration. As the warmer weather fades, herds of caribou must head south to survive the winter.

MIGRATION MYSTERY

At the end of the summer, the first severe thunderstorms signal that it is time for caribou to start moving to their winter feeding grounds. Caribou can change their migration routes from year to year, and larger herds go on longer migrations than smaller herds.

Caribou have broad feet that prevent them sinking into soft snow. They also use their hooves to shovel snow and reveal the tender lichen that survives underneath.

TIMELINE

SPRING

The herds head north to the tundra. There are no trees, and parts of the ground remain frozen all year. The journey north covers up to 965 km (600 miles).

SUMMER

The tundra bursts into life briefly and caribou feed on the grasses. Calves are born, then caribou move to windy shores or the foothills of mountains.

IN THE SUMMER, A CARIBOU CAN EAT UP TO 5 KG (12 LB) OF FOOD A DAY.

Male caribou have larger antlers than females. At the end of the summer, the males lock antlers with one another as they fight for mating rights, and often stop eating while they go through the mating season. A successful male might mate with up to 20 females.

Caribou cross roads, leap fences and swim across rivers to reach their destination. Calves are excellent swimmers, although pregnant females wait to give birth before attempting a tough crossing. **Calves can walk soon after birth, but can be at risk from wolves.**

Autumn
Spring

THE ROUND TRIP COVERS 5,000 KM (3,100 MILES).

AUTUMN
The first storms arrive, and caribou begin to trek south. They keep on eating and put on fat. They mate from September to November.

WINTER
The caribou are in their winter feeding grounds, but the weather is harsh and snow covers many of their food plants. Most animals lose weight, and in very bad weather, many may die.

GREY WHALE

CROSSING THE WORLD'S OCEANS

Where	Between the Arctic and Mexico
When	Spring and autumn
Why	For food and calving
How	Swimming

Grey whales make one of the world's longest migrations, from cold polar waters to warm tropical seas.

At the start of winter, grey whales leave the icy Arctic seas. It takes one of these whales just 55 days to swim 8,000 km (5,000 miles) to a Mexican lagoon to give birth. While there, the mother hardly feeds, but her newborn grows strong on its mother's milk – building up stamina for the return journey.

IN ONE YEAR, A GREY WHALE CAN MIGRATE UP TO 20,000 KM (12,400 MILES).

Russia
Chukchi Sea
Canada
Bering Sea
Pacific Ocean
USA
Mexico

— February–June
//// July–October
— November–January

MIGRATION MYSTERY

Grey whales set out on the journey south following a strict order. Pregnant females go first, then adult males, young females and finally the young males. It is a mystery how a whale calculates when it is the right time to leave, or how whales know the route they must follow.

FEBRUARY–JUNE

The whales leave their southern home for the journey north. Calves stay with their mothers and feed on milk as they swim. Most reach the Arctic waters by June.

JULY–OCTOBER

It is summer and some whales have reached as far north as the Bering and Chukchi seas. The Arctic waters are full of food, so the whales eat and put on

A WHALE CAN EAT UP TO 70 TONNES (77 TONS) OF AMPHIPODS IN THE SUMMER.

Like many other animals, grey whales spend the summer in the cold waters of the Arctic, where there is plenty of food for them. They feed mostly on amphipods – tiny sea creatures that they filter out of the water using baleen (special sieve-like plates) in their mouths.

Orcas (killer whales) follow grey whales to Mexico. Orca mothers show their young how to hunt the vulnerable newborn grey whales, separating them from their mothers before launching an attack.

Grey whales were hunted close to extinction. The populations in the eastern Pacific have recovered well, but there are **fewer than 100 whales left in the western Pacific population.**

A 45-YEAR-OLD WHALE HAS SWUM THE DISTANCE TO THE MOON AND BACK.

NOVEMBER–JANUARY

lots of fat, increasing their body weight by up to one-third.

The Arctic seas begin to freeze, so food is reduced. The whales depart on the journey south, swimming close to the shore for two months without stopping. When they arrive, the pregnant females give birth in the warm lagoons.

EUROPEAN EEL

SWIMMING AGAINST THE ODDS

Where	**Across the Atlantic Ocean**
When	**Throughout the year**
Why	**To lay eggs**
How	**Swimming**

One of the world's most extraordinary migrations is threatened, and may soon disappear forever.

European eels spend most of their lives in Europe's rivers, but one day they set off downstream towards the Atlantic. Most of them die before they get to the coast and the survivors then swim 5,000 km (3,100 miles) across the ocean. They travel for months, without resting or feeding, until they arrive in the Sargasso Sea, in the western Atlantic, where they mate and die.

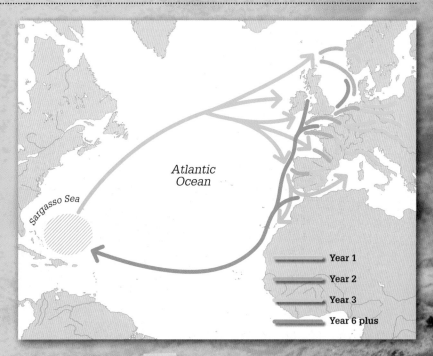

Atlantic Ocean

Sargasso Sea

Year 1
Year 2
Year 3
Year 6 plus

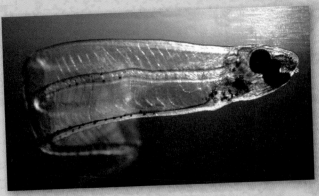

A newly hatched eel is called a leptocephalus. It is leaf-like in shape, tiny and transparent. Leptocephali swim with the Gulf Stream across the Atlantic Ocean and, while swimming, grow to 90 cm (35 in) long.

THE NUMBER OF EELS HAS FALLEN BY 99 PER CENT IN JUST 40 YEARS.

TIMELINE

YEAR 1

Between winter and spring, adult eels mate, lay eggs and die in the Sargasso Sea. Each egg hatches into a leptocephalus, which spends up to one year swimming back across the ocean. The tiny fish use water currents to help them on their migration. Many are eaten along the way.

Eels face many dangers. The destruction of their habitats and overfishing is a growing problem. They are also affected by parasites that have spread from Japanese eels, and water projects such as hydroelectric dams, that block their river routes. Predators, including seagulls, porbeagle sharks and pilot whales, hunt them in the ocean.

AN EEL CAN LAY UP TO 10 MILLION EGGS AT A TIME, BUT BREEDS ONLY ONCE.

The eel eggs hatch in the Sargasso Sea and the young eels spend the next year swimming back to the rivers where their parents lived. After more than ten years, eels return to the exact place where they hatched from eggs.

MIGRATION MYSTERY

For a long time, no one knew where European eels went to lay their eggs. Even now, their routes across the ocean and inland remain a mystery to scientists because most attempts to track eel migrations have failed. Scientists do know that silver eels can find their way to the Sargasso Sea even if they hatched from eggs on eel farms, and have never been to the ocean before.

YEAR 2

The leptocephali reach coastal waters and develop into glass eels. As they begin to migrate upstream into freshwater, they change again and are now called elvers.

YEAR 3

Eventually, the young eels reach the rivers inland where they will live for the next six to 20 years as they mature. They are now called silver eels.

YEAR 6+

In July, mature eels begin the journey downstream and head towards the ocean for the long journey home. Migrating males are usually six to 12 years old, and females are nine to 20 years old.

SOCKEYE SALMON

THE SALMON RUN TO BREED

Where	Pacific Ocean to Alaskan lakes
When	Spring and summer
Why	To lay eggs
How	Swimming

When sockeye salmon migrate, they have to battle past hordes of hungry predators, from sharks to bears.

This migration is called the 'salmon run'. As the fish head inland to their breeding areas in Alaska, predators lie in wait. The migration is both exhausting and dangerous; fewer than one in four sockeye salmon even make it to the river mouths past salmon sharks, sea lions and whales.

Sockeye salmon are blue when out at sea. However, when it is time for them to lay eggs, their bodies turn red, their heads become green and they return to freshwater rivers to mate. Males develop a humped back and a hooked jaw.

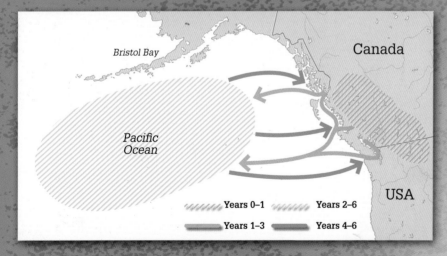

Bristol Bay

Canada

Pacific Ocean

USA

///// Years 0–1 ///// Years 2–6

—— Years 1–3 —— Years 4–6

MORE THAN 40 MILLION SOCKEYES MIGRATE THROUGH BRISTOL BAY IN ALASKA.

TIMELINE

YEARS 0–1

The sockeye salmon fry hatch from their eggs in winter in freshwater lakes or rivers. They are called alevins. At first, they feed on their egg sacs, then on insects that live in the water, and plankton (small floating animals and plants).

YEARS 1–3

Adult salmon migrate from their freshwater homes to the Pacific Ocean in the spring. As they travel, the colour and pattern on their bodies change so they are better camouflaged in the open ocean. Their kidneys also change, so they can cope with salty seawater. They are now known as smolts.

When the salmon migrate inland they must swim against river currents. Grizzly bears line the rivers, especially where the salmon fling themselves out of the water to leap over rapids and waterfalls. The bears lunge at the leaping fish with their jaws, or catch them in their massive paws.

MIGRATION MYSTERY

The strength of Earth's magnetic field changes from place to place. Salmon appear to have a 'magnetic map' and can sense these tiny changes in Earth's magnetic field. It is believed that they use this information to work out their position in the ocean, and change direction if necessary.

SOCKEYE SALMON TURN BRIGHT RED WHEN IT IS TIME FOR THE FEMALES TO LAY EGGS.

YEARS 2–6

The salmon move into the open ocean, feeding on small ocean creatures and fish. They can grow to nearly 90 cm (3 ft) long.

YEARS 4–6

Adult sockeye salmon return to the coast and head inland to the lakes where they were hatched. In June and July they mate, spawn (lay eggs) and die a few weeks later.

An alevin remains attached to its egg, which provides it with food. It stays where it hatched for up to 12 weeks over the winter while it grows. Some sockeyes never migrate to the sea, but they are much smaller.

DRAGONFLY

Where	From India to Africa
When	October to December
Why	To breed
How	Flying

Wandering glider dragonflies undertake the longest migration of any insect.

A wandering glider looks far too delicate to set off on a record-breaking journey. In fact, these fragile-looking insects complete a round trip of up to 18,000 km (11,200 miles). However, no one insect can do it alone – it takes four generations of dragonfly to complete the migration.

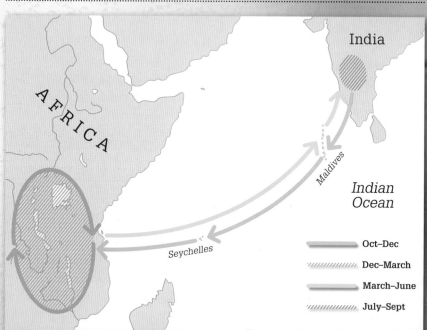

India

AFRICA

Maldives

Indian Ocean

Seychelles

————	Oct–Dec
/////////	Dec–March
————	March–June
/////////	July–Sept

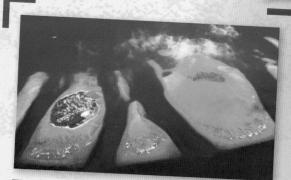

The dragonflies stop in the Maldives to feed. However, they cannot breed there because the islands are mostly waterless, so there is nowhere for the insects to lay their eggs.

THIS IS THE ONLY INSECT MIGRATION KNOWN TO TAKE PLACE OVER WIDE OCEAN WATERS.

TIMELINE

OCT – DEC

The first generation of dragonflies leaves southern India, and flies towards Africa, taking breaks in the Maldives and the Seychelles. Insects arrive at the stopovers in groups and stay for a few days.

DEC – MARCH

The dragonflies breed in East Africa, and the second generation continues the migration south, following the rains.

DRAGONFLIES CAN FLY AT HEIGHTS OF 6,300 M (4 MILES) BY GLIDING ON WINDS.

MIGRATION MYSTERY

A naturalist called Charles Anderson, who lives in the Maldives, discovered this dragonfly migration. He tracked the insects from Africa to India in the 1980s to work out their routes. Wandering gliders also migrate in North America, but no one knows where they come from or where they go.

Dragonflies lay their eggs in water, and their larvae live there. Most dragonfly larvae live in water for 10 to 11 months before changing into adults, then only live for another one to two months. Wandering gliders, however, spend just six weeks at the larvae stage and live most of their lives as adults.

With the wind behind them, the dragonflies can fly from India to Male (the capital of the Maldives) in less than 24 hours. The whole journey from India to Africa can be completed in four to five days. Birds such as kestrels (amur kestrel) and Kashmir rollers follow the insects on their migration.

A WANDERING GLIDER TRAVELS TWICE AS FAR AS A MONARCH BUTTERFLY.

MARCH – JUNE

A female dragonfly lays up to 2,000 eggs at a time.

The third generation of dragonflies begins the return journey towards India. They stop off at the Maldives for food. As there is no suitable place to lay their eggs, they soon move on.

JULY – SEPT

The final generation of dragonflies breed in India.

STRAW-COLOURED FRUIT BAT

A QUEST FOR FOOD

Where	Africa
When	November
Why	To feed
How	Flying

The sky turns dark when a colony of bats is on the move.

It has been described as one of the world's most incredible wildlife spectacles: at Zambia's Kasanka National Forest, 5,000,000 bats take to the air in just 25 minutes. The forest fills with the sound of shrieking, and the flurry of millions of flapping wings, as the colony of straw-coloured fruit bats leaves its roost to gorge on ripe fruit.

Oct–Nov Migration

Democratic Republic of Congo
Kenya
Tanzania
Angola
Zambia
Kasanka National Forest
Mozambique
Namibia
Zimbabwe
Botswana
Madagascar

Bats roost in large numbers in trees or caves. They sleep upside down, hanging by their feet, occasionally stretching their wings and 'chattering' to each other.

ONE BAT TRAVELLED 1,900 KM (1,200 MILES) IN ONE MONTH.

OCT – NOV

Vast numbers of bats appear at the Kasanka National Forest. Many of them arrive heavily pregnant, and need food – pregnancies can last from four to nine months.

NOV – DEC

The bats feast on the trees. They can eat up to twice their body weight in fruit every day. Pregnant females give birth and care for their young.

TIMELINE

MIGRATION MYSTERY

Bats are one of the most common – yet mysterious – of all mammal groups. They are difficult to study because they are often active after dusk and spend much of their time roosting in trees or flying. Scientists know very little about how many bats migrate, how they find their food or details of their migration routes.

Fruit-eating bats are also known as flying foxes because of their fox-like faces, with large eyes and snouts. Straw-coloured fruit bats are the second largest bats in Africa and have a wingspan of up to 90 cm (3 ft).

There may not be typical seasons in a tropical forest, but trees often flower and fruit at the same time. This means that plenty of food is on offer for monkeys, birds and bats. Migrating animals make the most of the feast by stripping the trees and then moving on to the next area where the fruit is ripe and ready.

UP TO 8 MILLION BATS MAY BE INVOLVED IN THIS MIGRATION.

JANUARY

Having stripped the trees, the bats begin their migration north. They can cover 1,000 km (620 miles) in a month. It is thought that many reach the Democratic Republic of Congo, or beyond.

FEB – SEPT

Straw-coloured fruit bats are found all over Africa. No one knows where the bats spend these months, or where migration routes start.

LEATHERBACK TURTLE

OCEAN MIGRATION OF ANCIENT REPTILES

Where	**Warm oceans**
When	**All their lives**
Why	**To feed and breed**
How	**Swimming**

Marine turtles first evolved around 200 million years ago, when dinosaurs were still alive.

Leatherback turtles migrate across an entire ocean, completing journeys of 1,000 km (620 miles) or more to reach their breeding grounds. They spend their whole lives at sea, but because they are reptiles they must lay their eggs on land. Marine turtles are in danger of extinction because they get caught in fishing nets, and people take their eggs for food.

Atlantic Ocean

Pacific Ocean

Indian Ocean

Pacific Ocean

Year 0–5
Year 5–10
Year 6–21

ONE TURTLE SWAM 20,557 KM (12,774 MILES) FROM INDONESIA TO AMERICA AND BACK AGAIN.

It takes a female leatherback turtle less than two hours to come to land and lay all her eggs.

TIMELINE

YEARS 0–5

Baby turtles hatch from their eggs on land and must dash towards the sea before they can be eaten by birds or dogs. Those that survive make their way out into the ocean and feed on plankton.

YEARS 5–10

The young turtles eat a range of animals, and follow currents into the ocean, covering vast distances as they mature. Adults eat jellyfish,

Male leatherbacks never come on to land, although they do come close to shore to mate. After mating, females clamber on to the beach, dig a hole and lay about 100 eggs before returning to the sea. When baby turtles hatch they must make their own way back to the sea.

MIGRATION MYSTERY

Many marine turtles return to the exact beach where they hatched, but leatherbacks are not quite so fussy and will lay their eggs on beaches nearby their 'home'. They probably find their way by staying with the ocean currents, which travel in large circles, and use a 'magnetic map' to fine-tune their route.

LEATHERBACKS CAN DIVE TO DEPTHS OF 1,280 M (4,200 FT) – DEEPER THAN ANY OTHER TURTLE.

BABY TURTLES FOLLOW THE MOONLIGHT TO FIND THEIR WAY TO THE SEA.

In parts of the Pacific, the population of leatherbacks has dropped by 90 per cent since the 1980s. Turtles have hard shells, but a leatherback's bony shell is hidden beneath a thick layer of dark leathery skin.

YEARS 6–21

but they often attempt to eat plastic bags by mistake instead – with deadly results.

The turtles become adults and are able to start breeding at any age between six and 21 years. They return to the area where they hatched to mate and lay eggs. After the breeding season, the adults return to the ocean.

ZOOPLANKTON

MIGRATING UP AND DOWN THE OCEAN'S DEPTHS

Where	All oceans
When	Every day
Why	To feed
How	Swimming

It is the world's tiniest creatures that complete one of the most surprising migrations.

Zooplankton are tiny animals that live in the sea. They spend most of the day lurking in the dark parts of the ocean, but rise towards the surface at night to feed. As morning comes, they sink into the deep again. Zooplankton might travel up to 1,000 m (3,300 ft) in just one day.

If this copepod were the size of a cheetah it would be moving at about 3,220 km/h (2,000 mph). For their size, some zooplankton are considered the fastest animals on the planet!

THIS IS KNOWN AS 'VERTICAL MIGRATION', AND IT IS THE WORLD'S LARGEST MOVEMENT OF ANIMALS BY MASS.

Zooplankton migrate for two reasons: to eat and to avoid being eaten. Tiny plants, called phytoplankton, live near the sea's surface where there is sunlight for them to photosynthesise. Zooplankton eat the phytoplankton, but so do larger animals, such as fish. By feeding at night, zooplankton are less likely to be eaten by bigger predators.

MIGRATION MYSTERY

The daily travels of zooplankton may be controlled by the light and dark patterns of day and night, but some plankton migrate even in the very deep ocean where there is no light at all. This suggests they may use a type of 'internal clock' too.

The quantity of animals in the sunlight zone increases by up to one-third during the night. Some zooplankton are too small to be seen with the naked eye.

CHRISTMAS ISLAND RED CRAB

SWARMING CRUSTACEAN TIDE

Where	Christmas Island
When	November to December
Why	To breed
How	Walking

This migration is timed by the movements of the Moon and ocean tides.

Christmas Island red crabs are land crabs that return to the sea to spawn. They live in dirt burrows in tropical rainforests, but when the rainy season comes, the crabs get the urge to move to the sea. Millions of them join the migration, crossing roads, climbing cliffs and facing predators on the way.

Christmas Island

Indonesia

Step 1 – migrate
Step 2 – mate
Step 3 – spawn
Step 4 – migrate

Australia

The crabs start their march as soon as the wet season begins. They need to move during the rains so their bodies don't dry out.

STEP 1 – MIGRATE

Adult crabs leave the forest any time between September and January. The migration takes about 18 days and the crabs stop to rest and eat along the journey.

STEP 2 – MATE

The crabs dig burrows, where they mate. The males return to the forest and the females stay in the burrows for 12–13 days while their eggs ripen.

All the females spawn (release their eggs) at the same time, before sunrise on spring tides during the last quarter of the Moon. This is when the difference between sea levels at high tide and low tide is at its lowest, making it safer for the baby crabs to hatch.

47 MILLION
RED CRABS MIGRATE TO THE SEA EVERY YEAR.

CHRISTMAS ISLAND IS HOME TO UP TO
120 MILLION
RED CRABS.

A young crab looks like a tiny prawn and is called a megalops. These red crabs live nowhere else on Earth. A crab can march up to 1 km (0.6 miles) a day. Each female releases up to 100,000 eggs at a time, but in some years no baby crabs survive their time in the sea.

MIGRATION MYSTERY

Most of the migrating crabs head towards the island's northwest shores. They walk in a straight line, but no one is sure how the crabs know where to go, or how the baby crabs know how to return to the forest when they emerge from the sea.

STEP 3 – SPAWN

In early January, all the females go to the sea and release their eggs at the same time. The eggs hatch into small swimming larvae immediately and the females migrate back to the forest.

STEP 4 – MIGRATE

After four weeks, the larvae have become tiny crabs, which emerge from the sea to migrate into the forest. This takes about nine days.

HALL OF FAME

MALI ELEPHANT

The elephants of Mali, in western Africa, survive the extreme heat of the desert by walking from watering hole to watering hole. These animals travel about 480 km (300 miles) every year from one source of water to another. It is the longest elephant migration known.

SPERM WHALE

Male sperm whales travel between the chilly waters of the Arctic and Antarctic around the two poles. The whales often swim in small groups. Once a year, they swim towards the equator to warmer seas where the females and young sperm whales live.

EMPEROR PENGUIN

Emperor penguins live in the sea but, like all birds, they lay their eggs on land. The penguins trek across the icy cold Antarctic terrain to breed and lay eggs. The male stays to protect the egg over the winter, while the female goes to the sea to feed and build up her strength. In spring, the female returns to meet the male and the newly hatched chick. The family then walks back to the sea.

ARMY ANT

Army ants keep on the move, building temporary nests rather than burrows. As they march, the ants collect all the food they can and kill every animal they come across. Worker ants carry young ants that are too small to march.

WHALE SHARK

Whale sharks are the world's largest fish and can grow to more than 10 m (33 ft) long. Up to 800 of them migrate annually to Mexico's Yucatan Peninsula. They can find enough food to last them for most of the rest of the year.

PRONGHORN

For thousands of years, enormous herds of pronghorns (deer-like animals) undertook 480 km (300 mile) journeys across Wyoming in North America. Some pronghorns still make this journey today, but they have to brave busy roads and railways.

WALRUS

Walruses usually follow the edge of the Arctic pack ice and migrate by swimming or hitching a ride on a floating piece of ice. Some Pacific walruses will travel up to 3,000 km (1,850 miles) every year as part of their journey through the Bering Straits between the Chukchi Sea and the Bering Sea.

GOLDEN JELLYFISH

The golden jellyfish of Palau's lakes in the western Pacific Ocean use the sun to guide their migration. Up to ten million jellyfish rise to the surface of the water at dawn and then follow the sunlight, moving across the lake during the day.

BLUE SHARK

The blue shark is often regarded as the most graceful of all sharks, with its sleek blue body and big eyes. These fish migrate in search of food and one shark is known to have travelled across the oceans covering nearly 6,000 km (3,700 miles) in a single journey.

BAR-TAILED GODWIT

Birds often migrate to warm places where they can raise their chicks. Bar-tailed godwits are some of the most impressive feathered travellers: one bird travelled across the Pacific Ocean non-stop from Alaska to New Zealand in just nine days.

GLOSSARY

CAMOUFLAGE
The way an animal is coloured or patterned so it is difficult to see.

COLONY
A group of animals, such as bats and ants, that live together.

COMPASS
Something that points to the magnetic north, and can be used to find the right direction.

CRUSTACEAN
A type of animal with no bones but a tough outer skin, and more than four pairs of legs.

CURRENT
Water that flows in a definite direction.

ECOSYSTEM
A group of animals and plants that live together in one place, and need one another to survive.

EXTINCTION
This is when a type of animal or plant has died out forever.

GULF STREAM
A warm ocean current that flows across the Atlantic Ocean.

HABITAT
The place where an animal or plant lives.

HERD
A group of grazing animals, such as antelopes or horses.

HIBERNATION
A long, deep sleep-like state that some animals spend the winter months in.

LAGOON
An area of salty water that is by the sea but often separated from it.

LARVA
The name for a young insect.

MATING
When a male and a female animal come together to make their young.

MIGRATION
A journey that an animal takes to find food, better weather, or a safe place to have young.

PARASITE
An animal that lives on another animal and harms it in some way.

PHOTOSYNTHESIS
The way that a plant uses the Sun's energy to make food from water and carbon dioxide (a gas in the air). In doing so, it releases oxygen, which we need to breathe.

PREDATOR
An animal that hunts other animals to eat.

PUPA
Some insects go through a big body change when they turn from larvae to adults. During this time they are described as a pupa.

REPTILE
A type of animal with scaly skin. Most reptiles lay eggs on land.

ROOST
A place where bats gather to sleep is called a roost. When a bat is hanging upside down to rest it is said to be roosting.

SPECIES
A particular type of animal or plant, such as the wandering glider dragonfly.

TOXIC
Something that is poisonous is described as toxic.

TUNDRA
This is a habitat found in cold parts of the world, where trees cannot grow and, underneath the surface, the ground is always frozen.

INDEX

Published in paperback in 2016
First published in hardback in 2015
Copyright © Wayland 2015

Wayland
An imprint of
Hachette Children's Group
Part of Hodder & Stoughton
Carmelite House
50 Victoria Embankment
London EC4Y 0DZ

All rights reserved.
Series editor: Elizabeth Brent

Produced by Tall Tree Ltd
Editor: Jon Richards
Designers: Ed Simkins and Jonathan Vipond

Dewey classification: 591.5'68-dc23

ISBN: 978 0 7502 9730 1
ebook: 978 0 7502 8758 6

Printed in Malaysia

Wayland is a division of Hachette
Children's Group, an Hachette UK company.
www.hachette.co.uk

10 9 8 7 6 5 4 3 2 1

Picture credits
shutterstock/BMJ, shutterstock/KA Photography
KEVM111, shutterstock/karamysh,
shutterstock/dcwcreations, shutterstock/NCG,
shutterstock/KA Photography KEVM111,
shutterstock/?, shutterstock/Arto Hakola,
shutterstock/Tony Brindley, shutterstock/ruj,
shutterstock/BMJ, shutterstock/Tory Kallman,
NOAA_anim2560/?, WIKI/Creative Commons
Attribution-Share Alike 3.0 Unported license, FLPA/
Jack Perks/FLPA, shutterstock/Vasik Olga,
shutterstock/bierchen, shutterstock/wilar,
shutterstock/Vishnevskiy Vasily, WIKI/Creative
Commons Attribution-Share Alike 2.5 Generic
license, shutterstock/Umkehrer, shutterstock/rinaK,
shutterstock/IrinaK, WIKI/Share Alike 3.0 Unported
license, shutterstock/aquapix, WIKI/Creative
Commons Attribution 2.0 Generic license, FLPA/
Stephen Belcher/Minden Pictures/FLPA